The Thinking Girl's Treasury of Real Princesses

Qutlugh Terkan Khatun of Kirman

© **2010 Goosebottom Books LLC**

Series editor **Shirin Yim Bridges**
Consulting editor **Amy Novesky**
Copy editor **Jennifer Fry**
Book design **Jay Mladjenovic**

Typeset mainly in Civitype FG and Volkswagen TS
Illustrations rendered in pen and watercolor

Some photographs used under Creative Commons Attribution/Share Alike license
http://creativecommons.org/licenses/by-sa/3.0/

Manufactured in Singapore

Library of Congress PCN 2010903713

First Edition 10 9 8 7 6 5 4 3 2 1

Goosebottom Books LLC
710 Portofino Lane, Foster City CA 94404

www.goosebottombooks.com

For Tiegan and Alena, the original Thinking Girl
and the real Fairy-Monkey Princess.

~ Shirin Yim Bridges ~

For my family and friends.

~ Albert Nguyen ~

The Thinking Girl's Treasury of Real Princesses

Hatshepsut of Egypt

Artemisia of Caria

Sorghaghtani of Mongolia

Qutlugh Terkan Khatun of Kirman

Isabella of Castile

Nur Jahan of India

Qutlugh Terkan Khatun of Kirman

By Shirin Yim Bridges | Illustrated by Albert Nguyen

goosebottombooks

She was called what?!

The names in this book can be hard to pronounce, and if you've ever heard Persian spoken, you'll know that an English pronunciation guide is not going to be of much help!

Here are most of the unusual names in this book, broken down so that you can say them. (Just don't expect to be understood by an Iranian person.)

Qutlugh Terkan Khatun	koot•look ter•khan kah•toon
Kirman	ker•mahn
Halal Khatun	hal•lal kah•toon
Il-Khanate	ill•khan•nate
Hulegu	hoo•lay•goo
Mongke	mong•keh
Sorghaghtani	sork•gak•tah•nee
Hajji Salih	ha•jee sah•lee
Ghiyath al-Din	ghee•yath al•din
Baraq Hajib	ba•rak ha•jib
Atabeg	ah•tah•beg
Yazd	yaz•id
Qutb al-Din	koot•ub al•din
Suyurghatmish	sigh•er•gat•mish

Qutlugh Terkan Khatun of Kirman

This story is going to sound like a fairy tale straight out of the Arabian Nights: a girl born into a noble family, in a faraway land torn by war, is taken in a raid by an enemy king and sold into slavery. In the squalor of the slave market, her sweet nature shines through and she is rescued by a kind merchant who brings her up as his own child. As she grows, her beauty, intelligence, and gentleness enchant all around her. So desirable is she that she is kidnapped again several times. Finally, she finds herself in the arms of a prince who marries her and makes her his princess. With him, she rules a nation. So wise and just is she, that on his death, the people ask her to continue as their ruler.

Now, doesn't that sound like a fairy tale? Yet, every word of it is true. And, as you'll soon see, there's even more to the story of Qutlugh Terkan Khatun.

Where she lived

Kirman, the territory that Qutlugh ruled, was one region of Persia (today's Iran), which was itself part of a greater area known as the Il-Khanate, ruled by Hulegu, the Il-Khan. The Il-Khanate was in turn part of the greater Mongol empire, all of which answered to Hulegu's brother, the Great Khan, Mongke.

The Mongol Empire

The Il-Khanate

Nepal

Saudi Arabia

India

Isfahan

Yazd

Kirman

When she lived

This timeline shows when the other princesses in The Thinking Girl's Treasury of Real Princesses once lived.

1500BC	500BC	1200AD	1300AD	1400AD	1600AD
Hatshepsut of Egypt	Artemisia of Caria	Sorghaghtani of Mongolia	Qutlugh Terkan Khatun	Isabella of Castile	Nur Jahan of India

Her Story

Qutlugh Terkan Khatun's birth name was Halal Khatun, which means "lawful princess or queen." Her family were nobles of Kirman (then part of Persia and now in southern Iran) and although they were not royal, you can guess from her name that they thought they should have been!

At that time, around 1220 AD, Kirman and the surrounding countries were in great turmoil. All the noble families were trying to topple one another for the chance to rule the new states forming under the Il-Khanate, the Persian part of the Mongol empire. Hulegu Il-Khan, brother of the Great Khan, Mongke, had recently conquered the area and was appointing princes to rule beneath him. (You can read more about how Hulegu and Mongke came to rule the world in the book about Sorghaghtani of Mongolia.)

The scrambles for power were vicious and violent, with the nobles of one city raiding those of another, setting fire to palaces and houses, killing the men, and carrying off the women and children to be sold as slaves. When she was just a young girl, Halal Khatun was captured in such a raid — torn away from her family to the screams of horses and the pounding of hoofbeats. (The rest of her family must have suffered a similar or worse fate, for she was never to hear from them again.)

Bundled away to the great city of Isfahan with its many mosques and minarets; deposited into the misery of the slave market; lost, lonely, and terrified; Halal Khatun somehow caught the attention of a passing merchant, Hajji Salih. Perhaps she was comforting the other children who were with her, holding their hands and soothing them in whispers as they sat roped together waiting to be sold like cattle. Maybe even then she radiated the concern for others that would one day become legendary. What we know for sure is that Hajji Salih saw something special in that little girl. With some effort, he found the money to buy Halal Khatun so that he could save her from a life of slavery, and he adopted her.

Hajji Salih made the rest of Halal Khatun's childhood as happy as he could. He loved her as his own child and saw to it that she was taken good care of, well dressed and well fed. He also made sure that she was well educated. (Persian women were often highly educated at that time, which was not the case for European women.) The reputation of Hajji Salih's adopted daughter soon spread. In the bazaars and souks the townspeople chuckled at stories about her lively intelligence. In the tea shops, sucking on their hookahs or water pipes, they marveled at her beauty as she blossomed into a young woman. But most of all, those who met her were touched by how this sweet girl had survived so much sadness.

In fact, the whole town was so enchanted by Halal Khatun that the chief magistrate decided he had to have this famous beauty for his wife. He began to court her, visiting Hajji Salih with gifts and sweets, hoping to negotiate a marriage. But Hajji did not approve of the self-important magistrate as a son-in-law. The magistrate's great pride was offended. Didn't Hajji Salih know who he was?! He decided to take Halal Khatun by force.

The townspeople sent word to Hajji, and in a night haunted by dark memories, Halal Khatun saddled up her horse and fled. She rode hard to the court of a neighboring prince, Ghiyath al-Din, to ask for the prince's protection. But on seeing this lovely young woman standing breathless before him, the prince fell in love with Halal Khatun himself. He insisted on marrying her, and Halal Khatun realized she had nowhere else to turn. So Halal Khatun married the prince, and became, as in her name, a real princess.

This mosque in Mashad, Iran, is said to have been built by Ghiyath al-Din. However, it was probably built in the 1400s — too late to be the handiwork of Halal Khatun's first husband.

However, the marriage was short-lived. Caught up in the continuing power struggles of the region, Ghiyath himself soon had to flee. (For some unknown reason, he didn't take Halal Khatun with him, although he did take his mother!) He was eventually killed by a rival, Baraq Hajib, the new ruler of Halal Khatun's birthplace, Kirman.

Even as her husband was being pursued to his death, word of the new princess' beauty spread. The princes warring over crowns and thrones now had another prize to fight for. Like little boys in a tug-of-war, the Atabeg (literally "father lord") of another great Persian city, Yazd, sent his army to seize her. Baraq Hajib, murderer of her husband, sent his army to keep her for himself. In the end, Baraq Hajib won. He took Halal Khatun back to Kirman and made her his wife.

This marriage did not last long either. A few years later, Baraq Hajib died and was succeeded by his dashing young nephew, Qutb al-Din. There was a custom at the time that a new king could inherit not only the throne, but a sweetheart or wife from the royal harem (for the sultans, khans, and atabegs all had many wives). It should come as no surprise that Qutb al-Din chose to inherit Halal Khatun.

◀ The Masjid Gate in the city of Kirman (also spelled Kerman), Iran, where Halal Khatun was born and where she eventually settled.

▶ The Imam Mosque in Isfahan, Iran, the city where Halal Khatun lived with her adoptive father, Hajji Salih.

What she wore

Hajib: a veil worn in public to hide the hair. This was often a simple rectangle of white cloth.

Clothing was worn in layers, with a cotton undershirt and underpants next to the skin.

Qutlugh Terkan Khatun probably considered herself a devout muslim. Her clothes would have reflected the teachings of the Koran in many ways. But like many other rich muslims, Qutlugh probably ignored the Koran's direction to avoid wearing silk, and to avoid wearing beautiful clothes that attracted attention. Miniature paintings from Persia around this time show many gorgeously embroidered robes and rich fabrics. Silk, which was first imported from China hundreds of years earlier, was a great favorite.

Several layers of long robes might be worn on top of each other. At least one of these robes would have had long sleeves. No skin was left exposed except for the head, hands, and feet. A pair of pants would also be worn underneath the robes.

The topmost layer was a long coat worn open in front. This was often richly embroidered. Although the Koran discouraged clothing that showed the body's shape, it became fashionable around Qutlugh's time to wear a long sash or scarf tied around the hips or waist.

The famous Persian art of miniature painting was developing during Qutlugh's lifetime. Persian miniature paintings were often used to illustrate books, or collected in albums to be enjoyed. They were highly detailed and very colorful.

This marriage to her Prince Charming — the first man apart from Hajji Salih to treat her as a human being and not just a prize or possession — was a long and happy one; so happy that Halal Khatun changed her name to Qutlugh Terkan Khatun, which meant "lucky and free princess." With Qutb's love and support, she was now in a safe place where she was free to be herself and to express her natural intelligence. Together, they had three children — a son and two daughters. And Qutb let it be known that Qutlugh was his partner in affairs of the state as well as those of the heart.

Qutlugh rewarded this trust. She proved herself so capable in government that she was given complete credit for all the good fortune and prosperity that befell both Qutb and Kirman. By the time Qutb al-Din died, 16 years later, Qutlugh Terkan Khatun was so well respected by the officials of the court, and so well-loved by the people, that nearly everybody wanted her to succeed him. The Il-Khan, Hulegu, agreed with their opinion. He officially placed all affairs of Kirman, both civil and military, under her control.

What she ate

Two sixteenth-century cookbooks survive from Persian courts. (One even has recipes contributed by different kings!) They indicate that Persian/Iranian cuisine hasn't really changed over hundreds of years. The recipes are not very different from Iranian recipes today, and are probably similar to recipes that Qutlugh would have used. They feature rice, meat, vegetables — especially eggplant, the "potato of Persia" — nuts, and dried fruits. The generous use of saffron shows that these recipes were meant for the wealthy. Saffron was an expensive spice then, as it is now.

But "nearly everybody" is not the same as "everybody." A group of nobles began plotting against Qutlugh, thinking that a woman, one who had not even been born royal, should not be on the throne. They sent a secret petition to Qutlugh's Mongol overlords, accusing Qutlugh of bad government and demanding her removal. But their accusations were quickly exposed as lies and the plotters were sentenced by the Mongols to be sent to the Il-Khan for execution. (The Mongols took loyalty very seriously.)

Now, until this point, Qutlugh Terkan Khatun had been celebrated primarily for her intelligence and wisdom. Since coming to power, she had been praised for being "extremely just ... the affairs of the kingdom of Kirman were kept in perfect order by her justice and equity." But from this point on, she would grow in fame for an even rarer and more valuable quality: compassion.

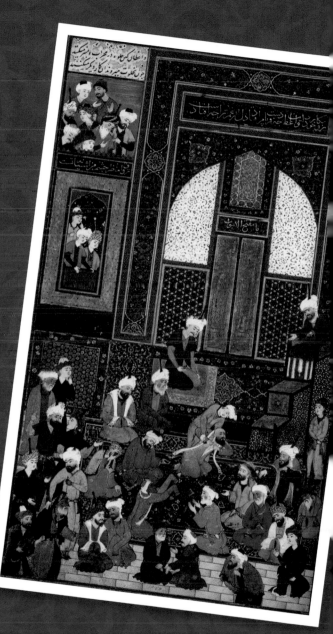

When she heard that her nobles had been sentenced to death, Qutlugh asked to take them to the Il-Khan herself. Was she going to watch the execution of the men who had plotted against her? (In those days executions were often treated as free entertainment. The Mongols were even known to build a temporary floor over sentenced men sewn up in sacks, so that by their dancing and carousing, they could squash their victims to death.) No. Once there, she pleaded with Hulegu for mercy. The Il-Khan was so moved that Qutlugh managed to bring home all the nobles unharmed.

Nor was this the last time Qutlugh had to deal with threats to her throne. At one point, her stepson Suyurghatmish (say that quickly three times!) tried to usurp power by establishing a rival court. After all, he was Qutb al-Din's son (by another wife) and felt he should have inherited the crown. Some nobles left the queen's service in order to join his. Once again, this episode ended in the prince and his nobles being sent to the Il-Khan for execution. Once again, Qutlugh asked for mercy for her enemies. This time, after issuing a decree that Suyurghatmish was no longer to meddle in Qutlugh's affairs, Hulegu found the prince and his nobles respectable new jobs, but doing things that had nothing to do with governing Kirman. (Suyurghatmish was very lucky to get whatever boring job he was given. As a prince, without Qutlugh's intervention, he would probably have been rolled up in a carpet and kicked to death or drowned in order to avoid the spilling of royal blood.)

Anybody who thinks that being merciful is a sign of weakness should learn a lesson from Qutlugh Terkan Khatun. Her compassion gave her an invaluable reputation. She rose in esteem not only in Kirman, but also in the Il-Khan's court. This former slave-girl was now so highly regarded that she was able to marry her favorite daughter to Hulegu's son, who would one day become Il-Khan himself. Qutlugh would be a welcome and frequent visitor to the imperial court for the rest of her life.

Qutlugh Terkan Khatun was to remain in power for 26 years. To this day, the period of her reign is considered to have been Kirman's golden age. This was the time of Kirman's greatest prosperity, when trade was brisk because highways were safe for all travelers and merchants; when land prices rose after years of warfare because of newfound stability and peace; when the lives of even the poorest peasants were improved by Qutlugh's generosity and care. She had water and drainage installed in villages, built and kept gardens in thousands of small towns so that the fragrance of roses sweetened the air, and provided cooking oil, wheat, and corn to be distributed to the clergy and the poor.

▲ Kirman has long been famous for its carpet weaving, and the trade that Qutlugh encouraged would have included the export of fine Kirmani carpets. Another major export for Kirman was (and still is) pistachios!

Her most touching act of compassion was discovered only after her death. When Qutlugh Terkan Khatun died from a high fever, her grieving family and friends found that the room next to hers was filled with piles of neatly folded clothes. In her last days, moving slowly to avoid bringing on the heart palpitations that had been bothering her, stooped and frail from her 70-plus years, Qutlugh had sorted out the clothes that she knew she would no longer need. With a trembling hand she had left instructions that these were to be given to women who had fallen on hard times. The less fortunate had been in the very last thoughts of this extraordinary princess.

▶ Qutlugh Terkan Khatun was buried under a cupola like this one, in the madresseh (Islamic religious school) that she had built in Kirman.